Going
Swimming

PaRragon

Bath · New York · Singapore · Hong Kong · Cologne · Delhi
Melbourne · Amsterdam · Johannesburg · Auckland · Shenzhen

Pages 6-7

Page 10

Pages 22-23

Page 8

Page 13

Pages 14-15

Page 26

Pages 28-29

Page 30

How to Use This Book

 Read the story, all about Olivia
going swimming for the first time.

 Look at each picture in the story closely.
You may be asked to find or count things
in a scene and place a sticker on the page.

 Try each activity as you go along, or read
the story first, then go back and do the
activities. The answers are at the bottom
of each activity page.

 Some pictures will need stickers to finish
the scenes or activities. Any leftover
stickers can be used to decorate the book
or your things.

Olivia's mom is taking her swimming in the big pool for the very first time. She has packed her backpack with everything she will need.

Can you find these things in the picture?

On the way, Olivia wonders if she'll like the big pool. "I've only ever been in the little pool," she says.

Find the sticker of Olivia to finish the picture.

"I'll be with you the whole time," Mom assures her. "It will be lots of fun!"

Which of these things are in the picture opposite?

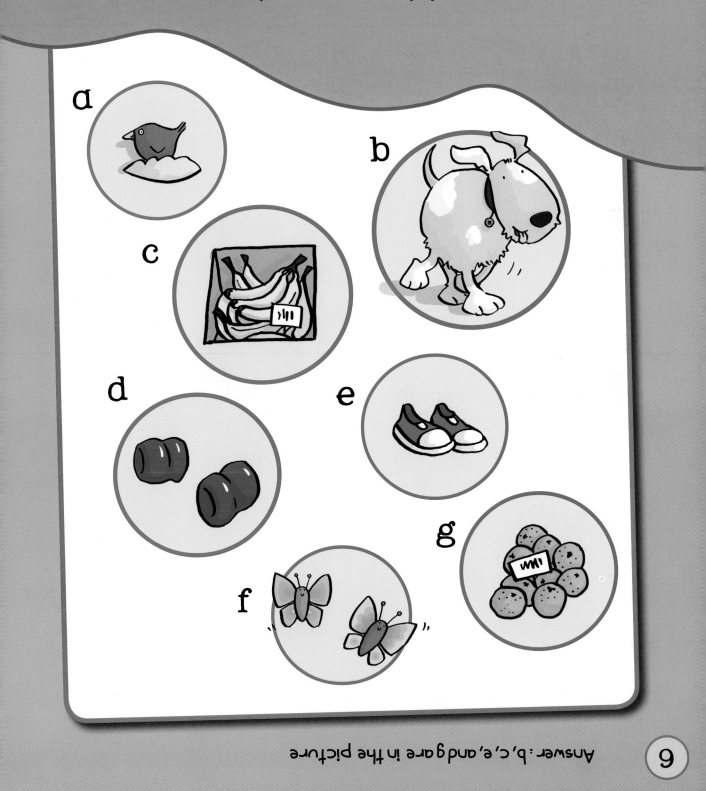

a

b

c

d

e

g

f

At the community center, Mom pays for two people for the swimming pool.

Find three stickers to finish the picture.

She gets a key for the locker, too.
"Thank you!" she says to the receptionist.

Look at the picture opposite
and see if you can answer
these questions.

1 How many people are
in the line behind
Mom and Olivia?

2 What color hats can you see?

3 Can you see two other
activities you can do at the
community center?

Time to get changed, but the swimsuits have gotten mixed up!

Follow the tangled lines to match Olivia and her mom with their swimming things.

In the locker room, Mom helps Olivia get into her swimsuit and arm floats.

Find two stickers to finish the picture.

They put their bags with their clothes, shoes, and towels in a locker for safekeeping.

Olivia can hear lots of splashing noises and laughing!

Now place the sticker of the lifeguard's life ring here.

No Running!

Olivia meets Bill, the lifeguard. His job is to make sure everyone stays safe.

"You'll be OK as long as I'm here," he tells her, smiling. "And I'm always here!"

Can you find five differences between this picture and the one opposite?

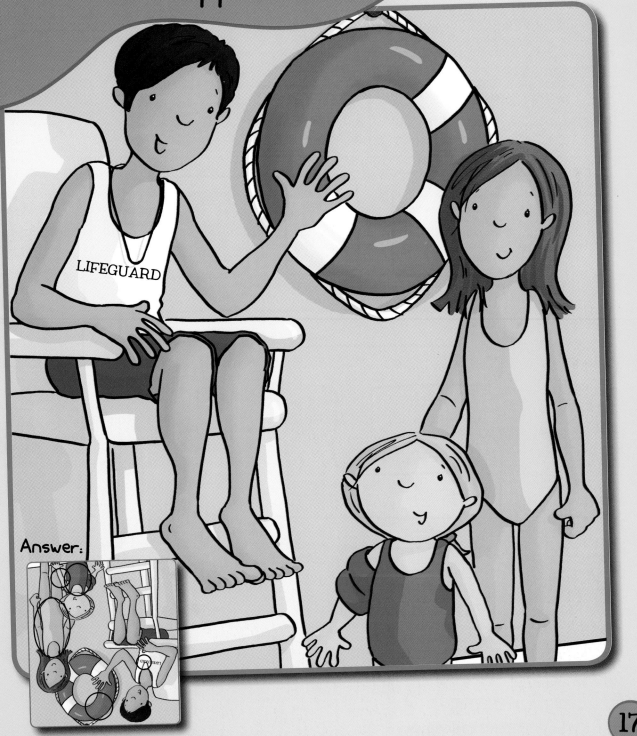

Answer:

Help Olivia and Mom find their way from the locker rooms to the swimming pool.

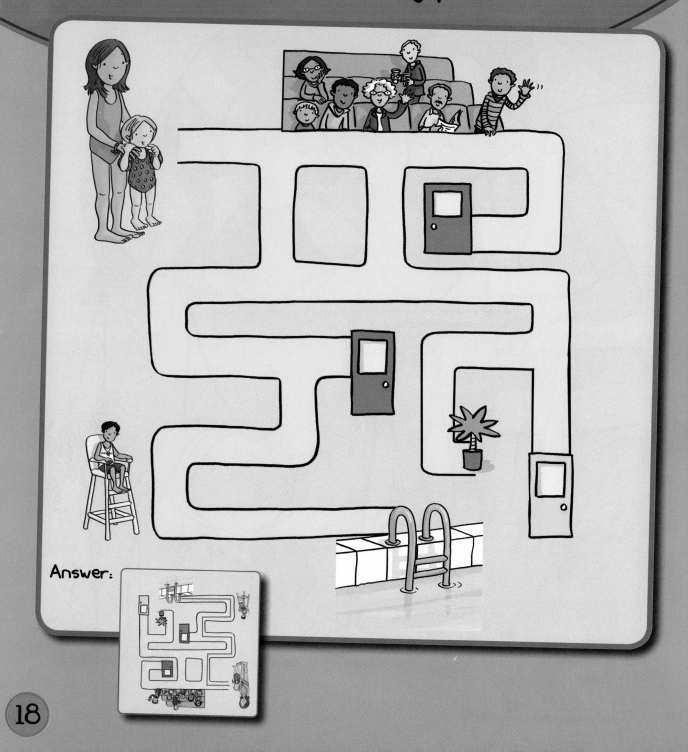

Answer:

Mom gets into the water first,
then she helps Olivia climb in.

"The water is nice and warm!" Olivia says.

Mom holds Olivia's hands, and
she floats in the water.

"I'm a mermaid!" shouts Olivia,
floating on her tummy.

Which two pieces complete the image below?

a

b

c

d

Answer: pieces a and c

Mom stays close by as Olivia lets go of
her hands and swims on her own.

Can you find these things in the picture?

 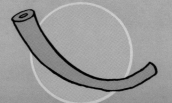 

"Look!" says Olivia. "There's Ethan and his mom!"

What color is Ethan's fish float?

Now place the sticker of Olivia here.

Ethan and his mom come and join them.
Everyone makes a circle holding onto
Ethan's fish float.

"We're dancing in the
water!" says Olivia, laughing.

Which picture exactly matches the one opposite?

All too soon, it's time to go. Mom helps Olivia climb out of the pool, then they have a shower and wash their hair.

Find two stickers to complete the picture.

Look at the objects below. Find one in each row that is different from the other two.

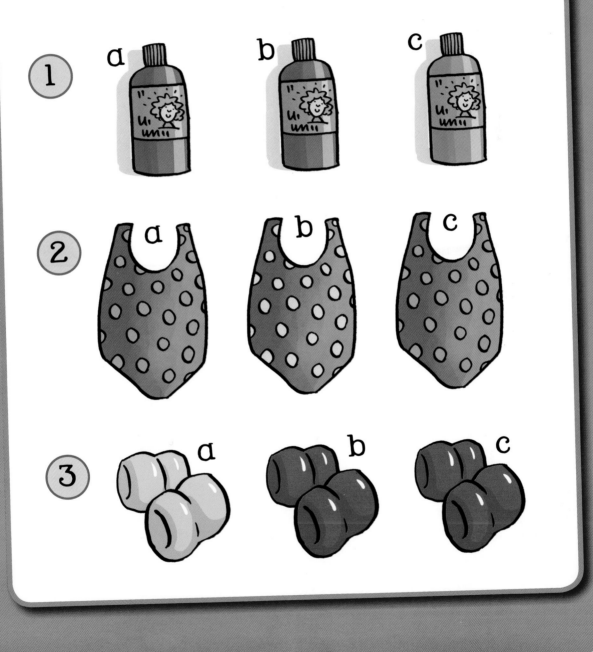

In the locker room, Mom uses the key to open the locker so they can get their stuff.

Can you find these things in the picture?

They get nice and dry,
and put on their clothes.

When they're dry and dressed, they meet
Ethan and his mom for a drink in the cafeteria.

Find the stickers
to complete
the picture.

"How did you like swimming?" Mom asks. "I loved
it!" Olivia said. "When can I come back?"